HOW TO BE FREE FROM SIN
WHILE SMOKING A CIGARETTE

Greg,

Thank you for
your hospitality!

Martin Zender

HOW TO BE FREE FROM SIN
WHILE SMOKING A CIGARETTE

The book for people with weaknesses

martin zender

Starke & Hartmann

How To Be Free From Sin While Smoking a Cigarette

Published by Starke & Hartmann
P.O. Box 6473
Canton, OH   44706
www.starkehartmann.com
1-866-866-BOOK

Printed in the United States of America

ISBN-13: 978-0-9709849-6-8
ISBN-10: 0-9709849-6-0

Cover model: Aaron Zender (who doesn't smoke, by the way)

To my mother

"For by faith are we walking,
not by perception."

—the apostle Paul
2 Corinthians 5:7

THE ROAD TO PEACE

I don't smoke, but I sometimes wish I did. I have other questionable habits that I won't burden you with. But I can picture myself holding a cigarette, or letting it hang cockeyed out of my mouth like Humphrey Bogart used to do. Whenever I talked—mumbled, I mean—the cigarette would bounce up and down. Then I'd squint and say something devilish to Lauren Bacall.

In this fantasy of mine, I know smoking is bad for me. I know it's wrong. I know I'm sinning, even while I'm doing it. But I do it anyway because it's cool, because life has been unfair to me, because Bacall has great legs, and because if I don't do *something*, I'll lose my mind. It's the worse kind of sin: knowing it's bad, but doing it anyway.

Preachers today lower their voices when speaking of such badness. They'll talk all sing-songy about stock sins like anger, jealousy, and pride. I call these stock sins because they're a dime a dozen. I'm not saying they're not bad, but I find myself doing them without even thinking. The sins I'm talking about—the sins that make the preachers furrow their eyebrows and talk like Vincent Price—are the ones where the wretched sinner says, "Yes, this would be a sin, all right," then does it anyway.

According to the clergy, there's no refuge for this. It's not like it's an accidental sin. It's not like it's a one-time deal. It's more like, "We're sorry, Lord, for what we did today. And we're sorry, too, that we're probably going to do it again tomorrow. And the day after that. And the day after that." The only comfort from the pulpit for this kind of badness is the remote possibility of a Sno-cone stand in hell. So no matter what your particular weakness is—

Well, hold on a minute. It just occurred to me that maybe you don't have a weakness. This is something I had not considered until now, and it changes everything. This project is shot if most of my readers don't have a weakness. If you don't have a weakness, how can I let you waste your time reading a book about weaknesses and how to deal with them? If you don't have a weakness, then please accept my apology, return this book to your bookseller, and use the money you saved to send a real sinner to Bible camp.

This book is written only for those who know what they're supposed to do but sometimes don't do it. It's written for those who think that their own particular weakness keeps God from completely liking them. It's written for those who just can't shake a bad habit. This book is written for the wretched souls who totter between their passion life and their desire for God, not realizing that in order to have a desire for God they must also be dogged by at least one detestable/wonderful passion that keeps them humble and needing Him. It was wrong of me to assume the worst of you. So forgive me, please, and have a blessed day.

For those who do have a weakness—or two—welcome to paragraph seven. It appears that we've lost a few of the religious folks. At least now we can speak honestly among ourselves.

"I just think it's funny that I've never had a weakness. Isn't that funny, Bill?"

We're believers. Or we're seekers. Some of us love Jesus Christ already; others aren't sure if we want to or not. In either case, there are bad things we all do occasionally (or continually, perhaps) that dismantle our happiness in front of God. They've got a term for this dismantling that is so weighty and terrible it deserves its own paragraph.

The term is guilt.

Is it possible to be free from sin, even while sinning? Is it possible to be free from sin and the guilt associated with it, even while narrowing your eyes at Bacall and leaning toward her match?

I know what religion has told you. Religion has told you that freedom from sin means you don't sin anymore. But is this God's thought? If this is God's thought, then no one today can be free from sin—at least none of the honest people who made it past paragraph six. But I generally find that God's thoughts and the thoughts of orthodox religion are two different things. I'm happy to report it's the case here.

This book is written and dedicated to all the poor sinners in the world who can't stop sinning, but who love or want to love the Lord, Jesus Christ. Here's the good news: *You have already been freed from sin.*

Thanks for hanging on. God's Word is about to deliver you from discouragement, condemnation and guilt, without asking you to change a thing you're doing. On second thought, you may have to change one thing. If you've been beating yourself over the head trying not to sin, you're going to have to quit that. Stop assaulting your head.

You still here? Great. That last paragraph wasn't a joke. I would never joke about something as serious as sin. How could I possibly tell you to quit pummeling yourself over it? Because this monumental effort—and the repeated failures and inevitable guilt trips that follow—is ruining your opinion of yourself, taking away your peace, and robbing you of the affection due Christ. You're working so hard trying to *impress* Him that you're not paying enough attention *to* Him.

"But if I let down my guard for even a second," you say, "I'll sin like a crazy person."

Hold on. That's what religion has told you, and I just suggested that religion is usually wrong. It's wrong here, for sure. Religion supposes that by keeping a moral watchdog chained to your flesh, you'll stop sinning. You've probably already disproved this theory with many a botched New Year's resolution. The Pharisees disproved it two thousand years ago.

Pharisees 101

The Pharisees of Jesus' day tried hard to stamp sin from their lives. The result? They sinned like crazy people. What a paradox. But you've proven it in your own life: the more you try not to do the thing you hate, the more you think about the thing you hate, and the more you do it. God is quite aware of this principle and—if you can believe it—He invented it. He made us this way on purpose in order to drive us in helpless frustration to His dispensary of grace. Don't take my word for it; it's Romans 5:20, and the entire seventh chapter of that amazing book. I will dig into these scriptures for you later, and you'll jump for joy when you read what the apostle Paul has to say there. I know that's a cliché—jump for joy—but if you literally do it, it won't be a cliché anymore.

Back to the Pharisees. They looked all their lives for Messiah, and tried to look pretty for Him when He came. Then He did come; He stood so close to them they could smell the fish on His breath and touch His dusty clothes. And they hated Him. They hated Him, slapped Him, ripped His clothes off and killed Him. That's what religious zeal will do to you. It squeezes you with the worst kind of pressure (the pressure required to fix yourself

for God) and makes you so crazy and blind that you want to kill a person who picks corn on the Sabbath and exudes great joy. At the very least, it discourages you so badly (because you'll never be perfect) that you'll want to smoke cigarettes (if that's your particular weakness) until you die.

The great tradition continues

Most Christian institutions today employ Pharisee-type leaders. The only difference is that the modern Pharisees wear nicer shoes, whitewash their programs with Christ's name, and don't realize they're Pharisees. Take Jim Bakker and Jimmy Swaggart, for instance. These men, former pillars of the Christian institution, came down hard on sin. The seminary trained them that way: don't do *this*, and shame on you for *that*. Then what happened? Sin came down hard on them. Swaggart swore off women with red-faced determination, turning red again later for different reasons. Same with Bakker. The only difference between these people and millions like them is that these made headlines.

Look what happens to the kids of clergy, generally. As soon as they get out on their own, they come undone. Some dye their hair green; others merely give up on God. What's the problem? This: the clergy today, like the clergy of yesteryear, is still trying to fix itself, to fix its children, to fix you, and to sanitize the world for Christ. Sounds good, doesn't it? Well, no. It's a recipe for moral disaster.

Let go and let God

You may not believe this yet, but "let go and let God" is scriptural advice. Yet no Christian I've ever met follows the advice. Let go and let God? Hm. With them, it's more like, "Hold on tight and win one for the Deity."

What pastor would ever tell you to let go, and mean it? No institutionally trained clergyman I've ever heard of trusts grace. Instead, the clergymen bind their flocklings with moral watchdogs, not the least of which is the Ten Commandments. They don't want to have to pick their people up off the street corner some day, and they think that the Law of Moses (a "dispensation of condemnation," 2 Corinthians 3:9) will prevent it. But I'm telling you that letting go and letting God is the only advice that will keep these people from that corner. I say let the pastor be the one who will eventually crack up—because he will.

What's that? You say you know a couple friends who really do seem to live sinless lives? You say they'd make good candidates for the cover of *Virtue* magazine? They seem so together? And when you ask them about their idyllic walk, they answer with a verse and a smile? They never seem desperate, ruffled or disturbed? You can't picture them throwing a loaded coffee mug against the wall, cursing, or crying out their complaint to God? Yeah. I know the type. Complaining is a sin, so they would never do it. And things seem to go well for them most of the time, right? Yes, I know. I know just the kind of people you're talking about. But there might be the key to their behavior: things seem to go well for them most of the time. I've noticed that what often passes for the Christ life in Christian circles today is in reality a supreme level of self-control in a life untested.

Will the real Job please fall down

Before his trial, scripture describes Job as "flawless and upright." This is verse one of chapter one. But then Job loses his family, his wealth, and his health. Now listen to him in chapter ten, verse one: "My soul is disgusted with my life; let me give free rein to myself and my concern; let me speak in the bitterness of my soul." Ah, there's the real Job, the mess of a man that was seething beneath that skin all along. But before he could understand his weakness, Job had to be broken. Can you imagine your Christian brother or sister even thinking Job's "blasphemous" words? No one would invite the real Job to the Wednesday prayer meeting, at least not without asking him to comb his hair and keep his scabby mouth shut.

George Bernard Shaw was a genius. It was he who said: "Virtue is insufficient temptation." Many times, those who appear virtuous have not been sufficiently tempted. Their virtue is Hollywood-wall virtue, propped up with half a dozen two-by-fours and a New Year's resolution. It's self-control un-tested. The world can spot phony Christian virtue ten miles away. Christians can't see it because they are too busy admiring themselves in the mirror.

Real human virtue is being broken by trial and ly-ing like a pile of lumber in the wake of a hurricane. That's when the good stuff starts; it's when God goes to work. Real human virtue is helplessness before God. Helplessness before God is the beginning of a true spiri-tuality that stands strong when the wind blows. Well, it has no place to go but up.

Swinging free

I don't expect the modern religious hierarchy to care much for this book. You're about to get freed, and that scares them. It may even scare you—at first. It may scare you to drop the Ten Commandments (they weren't de-signed to produce morality anyway, but rather to drive you in helplessness to Christ), to dump the New Year's resolutions, to let go and trust grace. As I said before, "let go and let God" doesn't sound like very scriptural advice. But there's a whole chapter of Scripture (rarely read or understood) dedicated to explaining it. In the end, it's the only thing that works.

This kind of happy walk may seem to you like hang-ing by your knees from a trapeze, without a net. But just think how great your hair will feel, swinging free like that. Besides, more trapeze artists fall *with* nets than do those without them.

Aren't the arms of Christ better than a net anyway?

WHO WE REALLY ARE

As people of faith, our walks are up and down. Yesterday we had victory over sin, today we didn't. Tomorrow we might, depending on what Sheila wears to the office, or how the bakery smells on the way home. If God reckoned His favor of us according to our walks, He'd be dizzy. But it's we who get dizzy, not Him. The challenge is to see ourselves as God sees us.

Nothing can be said here without considering the cross. The cross of Christ is why sin can't condemn us. The cross of Christ is why I can sit here in front of a computer monitor and write about it, while eating a Tootsie Pop. Without the sacrifice of Christ, sin separates us from God. But because of it, we are delivered from Sin's condemnation even while caught in its clutches. In other words, we learn its lessons now without feeling its lash. These are all just fancy ways of saying that we are free from sin while smoking a cigarette.

To those still struggling with the guilt, condemnation and discouragement that comes from being a sinner, I have these three things to say to you:

- You feel condemned, while God sees you as justified (Romans 5:9)
- You're waiting for the lightning bolt, while God's thoughts of you are of peace (Romans 5:10)
- You fear for your salvation, while God is not reckoning sin to your account (Romans 4:8)

Because of Christ's work, God's disposition toward you is sunshine—2 Corinthians 5:19. All cumulonimbus clouds are on your side of the windowpane.

Let's try something now that few have ever attempted. As we begin this next section, let's take our eyes off of ourselves. Let's stop worrying about what we're doing for God and start appreciating what God has done for us. Before we can do this, however, we will have to lose our religion.

DREAD-TEACH, and how

Religion is the biggest hindrance of all to appreciating freedom from sin. Whenever people tell me they "got religion," I pray for them and send them a packet of Rolaids.

I have yet to give you my definition of religion, though you probably suspect that I don't much care for it. You're right. Religion has ruined a lot of decent people, turning them into self-righteous nincompoops.

Religion and truth are as opposed as can be. Religion is man standing on his head for God; truth is God standing on His head for man. Religion stands tall and says, "Look what I'm doing for God;" truth takes to its knees and says, "Look what God has done for me." Religion is man keeping track of his walk, watching himself, preparing himself, trying to make himself presentable to Jesus; truth is man sitting down, giving up, and watching a singular act on a hill called Calvary. Religion is man; truth is God. Religion crucified Jesus Christ; truth raised Him.

> RELIGION IS MAN STANDING
> ON HIS HEAD FOR GOD;
> TRUTH IS GOD STANDING
> ON HIS HEAD FOR MAN.

Millions have been tortured, imprisoned and killed in the name of religion. It fits. The elements of the Greek word translated "religion" (*deisidaimonia*), in the Concordant Literal New Testament are "DREAD-TEACH." Disgruntled churchgoers will appreciate that literal definition. The word "religion" itself comes from a Latin root, *lig*, which means "to tie or bind." This is suggestive of a person restrained by a system of worship, unable to get up and wander out to the meadows and mountaintops where Christ is.

The powers of darkness back every religion on earth, including the one we're considering in this section. The bad guys aren't wearing black, folks. Satan, today, is disguised as an angel of light:

> For such are false apostles, fraudulent workers, being transfigured into apostles of Christ. And no marvel, for Satan himself is being transfigured into a messenger of light. It is no great thing, then, if his servants also are being transfigured as dispensers of righteousness—whose consummation shall be according to their acts (2 Corinthians 11:14).

Organized crime is one of many obvious evils in the world, but religion has claimed far more victims—people who have literally worried themselves to death dreading God, straining to meet His standards, then damning themselves for failing Him. What a crime. What an evil. Indeed, religion is the best cloak evil ever had.

The powers of darkness want people ignorant of God, and they accomplish this by engaging men and women in the needless exercise of working to win God's affection. Religion demands that people "walk the line" to win the affection of a God Who already could not possibly love them more. The powers of darkness can do nothing to deny God's present benevolent attitude toward humanity, but they can do plenty to keep people from knowing about it.

The "gospel" in the churches today is no gospel at all. It's a call to personal and social activism that engages the affections with sin, self and sanitation: we must do away with sin, we must control ourselves for Jesus (known in Christian camps as, "dying to self"), we must sanitize the world for Christ. As for the glories of the One seated above, we'll get to those after the rally at the statehouse–maybe.

Morality campaigns in churches today are displacing Colossians 2:10, which says that we are complete in Christ. I'm not saying there is no place for instruction in the living arts. I am saying that knowledge of self in our modern churches is substituted for knowledge of God and Christ. The cross was Christ's message that self is finished, yet the Christian message today is self's new beginning. It's the digging up of the corpse of the old humanity that Christ buried at Calvary.

Yet scripture is a revelation of God's work, not ours.

Freedom from sin, therefore, has to do with what Christ did, not with what we are doing. Otherwise, we could never be free from sin. The recurring theme of this book, which I will illustrate in several ways, is this: *What you do has no effect on who you are in Christ.*

This is how you can be free from sin. Isn't that a relaxing thought? I'm about to show you how true it is.

When were we justified?

I hope it never happens to you, but there could come a time in your life when you trip on a sidewalk seam, fall down, and bump your head on a fire hydrant. Or, worse, you could join a religion. The ensuing brain trauma in either case could cause you to think that you're somehow worthy of your salvation, and that you're expected by God to maintain it. To ensure that victims of such disasters could be reacquainted with the facts, God

"I got hit by a truck yesterday and now I'm obeying the Mosaic Law. Hell, I should have just joined a religion."

wrote Romans 5:8. He wrote this so that people would know without a doubt that they're finished before they start, and that they have nothing to do now but relax and thank Him. Unfortunately, people have to read this verse to appreciate it. Apparently, not many have done it.

Romans 5:8—"Yet God is commending this love of His to us, seeing that, while we are still sinners, Christ died for our sakes."

God went out of His way here to say, in effect, "I did not justify you in your Sunday clothes. I did not justify you while you were loving your neighbor as yourself, or praying to Me in the quietness of your room. Instead, I justified you while you were yelling at your children, running up your credit card, stuffing yourself with donuts—and worse. I did this for you on your worst day, not your best. I did it this way so that you could thank Me the rest of your life instead of wasting your time trying to figure out how to downplay your faults and impress Me."

What did you say, God? Our robes were rustling.

When God justifies us this way, we're finished before we start. Since He did His best for us at our worst, what can we do now to improve the relationship? Act better? But He already did His best for us while we were acting our worst. What can we do now to blow our relationship with Him? Sin? But He already maxed out on His love for us while we were sinning like crazy people.

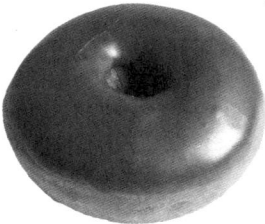

The photograph

You're the father of a teenage son. One Saturday morning at 2 a.m., your son returns home drunk. He wakes you up because he knocks over a lamp trying to get through the living room. He's trying to work his way down the hall now, but you switch on the hall light and freeze him like a startled deer in the headlights. Jimmy's hair is disheveled and there is vomit on his shirt. He puts one arm out against the wall to support himself, avoiding your gaze by staring at the floor. "Hey, Dad," he manages to say. All Jimmy wants is to go to bed. He makes a move toward his room, but you work yourself between him and the door.

"Hang on a minute, Jim."

You wonder if you should awaken your wife, but Beth is already standing at the doorway of your bedroom, arms across her chest. Now is when the inspiration strikes. With Beth and Jimmy wondering what's going to happen next, you retrieve your camera from the hallway closet. Engaging the flash button, you wait for the orange light. When everything's ready, you hand the camera to Beth, walk over to Jimmy, put your arm around him with a big smile and say, "This one's going to be just you and me, Jim. Beth, take the picture." Jimmy's chin is still on his chest, but your smile broadens as the flash pops. Jimmy thinks you've lost your mind;

Beth isn't too sure about you either. Oh, well. Tomorrow's another day.

Ain't it though. The following day, you print the picture. *This is your son.* He is bone of your bone, flesh of your flesh, and you love him. You take the picture to work. The first person you look for is your boss. "Mr. Spencer, this is my son and me. He's my oldest boy. I love him more than anything in the world." On the subway on the way home, you're inspired to pull out the picture and show it to your seatmate, a total stranger. "Do you have a son? I do. Here. This is me and my oldest boy, Jimmy. I love him more than I love myself. I would die for this young man!" There are tears in your eyes.

This is precisely how God shows us off in front of the universe.

This is why we are now free from sin.

Who we are vs. what we do

Here is some pressure-relieving news: What we do has no effect on who we are in Christ. Don't thank me, thank God for sending His Son to justify you in your worst condition, not your best. He did not merely make it possible for you to be saved at that cross, He saved you then. The cross wasn't some piece of groundwork Christ laid that now requires your belief to validate it.

No. You were saved at that cross two-thousand years ago, and all that now remains is for God to acquaint you with this fact at some point during the course of your life. You believe because you are saved, you are not saved because you believe.

There's a Christian saying that goes, "God did it. I believe it. That settles it." This saying contains one too many sentences, namely the one in the middle. Remove the middle sentence and the phrase becomes scriptural. If you have to, tack the middle sentence onto the end, like a caboose. Whatever you do, don't put it between "God did it," and "that settles it." That's blasphemy.

Adam and Christ

All humanity boils down to two individuals: Adam and Christ. If you want to comprehend the race, you need only comprehend these two, for they represent the whole. No need wasting time studying anthropology, mankindology, or whatever other "ology" they're offering at universities these days. Read the next few paragraphs and you'll have mankind in the bag. Everyone besides Adam and Christ can clear out of the ring, buy popcorn and sit down.

Scripture plays Adam and Christ against one another many times, while the rest of mankind sits breathlessly (and helplessly) in the shadows. This revelation dethrones the pride of many, and I do love it when that happens. But neither our wonderful works nor our horrible sins could ever affect our ultimate destiny—*that* is decided by the work of two, and two alone.

In this corner...

Watch and learn from these scriptural bouts between Adam and Christ.

Romans 5:18: "Consequently, then, as it was through one offense for all mankind for condemnation, thus also it is through one just award for all mankind for life's justifying."

Romans 5:19: "For even as, through the disobedience of the one man, the many were constituted sinners, thus also, through the obedience of the One, the many shall be constituted just."

1 Corinthians 15:22: "For even as in Adam, all are dying, thus also, in Christ, shall all be vivified."

As the revelation sinks in, a reader complains: "It's not fair that I was condemned in Adam."

This is the common complaint leveled at God after folks discover that, because of Adam's transgression, they're doomed to eighty or so years of paying bills and burying relatives.

"It's not fair," says the reader again. "I wasn't even there."

So you weren't.

"*I* didn't sin like Adam."

So you didn't.

"Why should *I* be included in the condemnation of that disobedient man?"

Good question.

"*I* didn't line up for it. Did anybody ask me? I don't recall anybody saying, 'Excuse me, sir, would you like to be included in the condemnation of Adam?' This thing happened before I was born, but now, *I'm* stuck with it. Now *I* have to earn my bread by the sweat of my brow."

It's a rough way to go, I'll admit that. A crying shame. Bread should come easier than this. How does your wife feel about it?

"Cindy? Not good. Because of Eve, she has had to bear tremendous pain in childbirth. While our last child was being born, I made the mistake of asking Cindy what it felt like. She grabbed my throat, dug her fingernails into my neck, pulled my ear next to her mouth and said, 'If you want to know the feeling, *Gary*, grab your bottom lip and pull it over your head.'"

I understand your complaint, Gary, I really do. But now listen as I address the readers again and flip this coin over.

Gary was right. Without asking them, God included Cindy and him under the curse of Earth's inaugural human. They weren't there in the garden; they didn't eat the forbidden fruit. Nevertheless, under Adam they went. Because remember: all mankind is wrapped up in Adam and Christ. Because of Adam, all are condemned. But because of Christ, all will be justified.

I just flipped over the coin. I did it quickly; did you see it? You already read about it in Romans 5:18-19 and 1 Corinthians 15:22. Everyone condemned in Adam will be justified in Christ—*and this isn't fair, either.* None of us asked for it; none of us hung on that cross. Yet because of the Greater Man's work, everyone constituted

All justified.
No fair

a sinner in Adam will eventually be constituted just in Christ. Have you escaped condemnation in Adam? Only then can you escape justification in Christ.

Does everyone experience this justification simultaneously? No. Just as a person cannot experience Adam's curse until he or she is born, neither can a person experience Christ's victory until Christ chooses to reveal it to him or her. But it will happen for every son and daughter of Adam, if not in this life, then in the next. This is the testimony of scripture:

1 Timothy 2:5-6, "For there is one God, and one Mediator of God and mankind, a Man, Christ Jesus, Who is giving Himself a correspondent Ransom for all, *the testimony in its own eras.*"

1 Corinthians 15:22-23, "For even as, in Adam, all are dying, thus also, in Christ, shall all be vivified. *Yet each in his own class.*"

The same all who are dying in Adam will be vivified (that is, be given life beyond the reach of death) in Christ. Once again, if you have escaped condemnation in Adam, only then can you escape the result of the cross. The three scriptural bouts I showed you between Adam and Christ are perfect parallels. Man's theology, however, has destroyed the parallels, placing everyone under Adam's

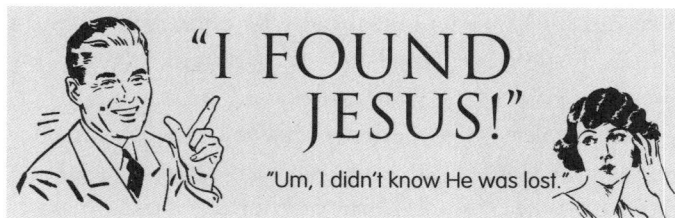

"I FOUND JESUS!"

"Um, I didn't know He was lost."

disobedience, but only a fraction under Christ's obedience. Man's theology has made the former involuntary, while the latter they have made a matter of free choice. Scripture doesn't do this, man does. By doing so, man's theology has made Adam greater than Christ.

This does not seem to bother anyone.

Someone once said to me: "I found Jesus."

"That's interesting," I answered. "I didn't know He was lost."

Many claim that, while they never chose Adam, nevertheless they do choose Christ. I understand that these people *feel* like they chose Christ, but in reality, Christ chose them. Jesus told His disciples, "Ye have not chosen Me, but I have chosen you" (John 15:16). I believe Jesus knew what He was talking about.

In Adam, all our righteousness was as filthy rags; that's Isaiah 64:6. No matter what good we did in Adam, we couldn't break out. Frustrating and unfair? Sure. But now turn the coin over. But be careful, because here is where many people lose track of the parallel. As none of our righteousness counted in Adam, none of our sin counts in Christ. I know that sounds radical, and it is. The cross was radical. We still reap what we sow in the flesh, but this righteousness/sin thing is a *spiritual* principle, not a fleshly one: sin cannot now separate us from the love of God.

No fair.

Now you see him, now you don't

Since I'm taking you so far from orthodoxy's doorstep, I'll give you a practical illustration of this truth from Scripture.

Romans 7:2-3:

> For a woman in wedlock is bound to a living man by law. Yet if the man should be dying, she is exempt from the law of the man. Consequently, then, while the man is living, she will be styled an adulteress if she should be becoming another man's, yet, if the man should be dying, she is free from the law, being no adulteress on becoming another man's.

Here we have a woman bound to a man by marriage. If, while her husband is alive, she shacks up with another man, she's styled an adulteress. Yet, if her husband dies while she's with the other man, she's not an adulteress.

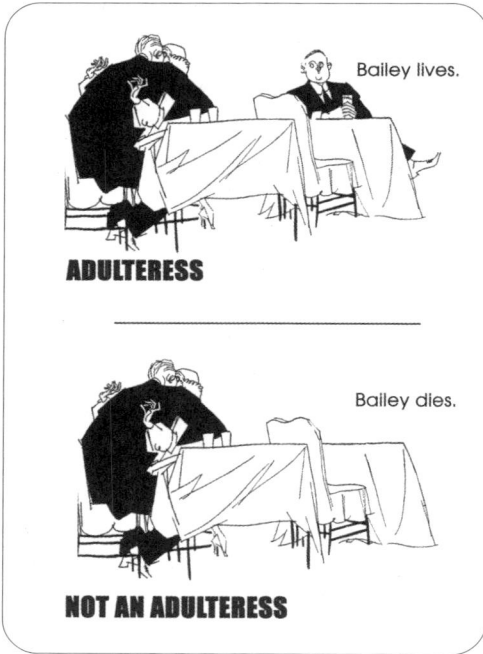

Let's call the woman Leona and the illicit lover Leroy. In both cases, Leona shacks up with Leroy. This is the common denominator; nothing changes on Leona and Leroy's side of the equation. In Paul's example, whether this woman is styled an adulteress or not depends, not upon what she or her lover does, but upon what a third party does, namely, her husband Bailey.

In the top example above, Leona is an adulteress. In

the bottom example, she isn't one. What changes on Leona's side of the equation? Take a close look. The answer? Nothing. In both cases, she's shacking up with Leroy. Or, in Paul's language, she is "becoming another man's." What, then, makes the difference between whether Leona is an adulteress or not? *The action of another man*, namely, her husband Bailey. While Bailey is alive, Leona is an adulteress. When Bailey dies, she's not an adulteress. The thing that changes everything is the action of Bailey.

Now apply this to us and Christ. Here's how it works:

"Consequently, then, as it was through one offense for all mankind for condemnation..."--Romans 5:18

"...thus also, it is through one just award for all mankind for life's justifying..." --Romans 5:18

CONDEMNED

This is the sinner, Edmund, in Adam.

"Through one man, sin entered into the world"--Romans 5:12.

JUSTIFIED

This is the sinner, Edmund, in Christ.

"While we are still sinners, Christ died for our sakes. Being now justified in His blood, we shall be saved from indignation"-- Romans 5:8-9.

In the example at left on the previous page, Edmund is a sinner. In the example on the right, he's still a sinner. What changes on Edmund's side of the equation? Nothing. In both cases, Edmund is a sinner. What, then, makes the difference between whether Edmund is considered condemned or justified? Is it anything he does? No. The action of two representatives, namely, Adam and Christ, determines whether Edmund is either condemned or justified.

Apply it personally now. As long as we're in flesh, we're sinning. While we're sinners in Adam, we experience condemnation. But while we're sinners in Christ, we experience justification. What changes on our side of the equation? I've repeated it many times, but the answer is a seven-letter word that begins with "n" and ends with "g." The answer is "nothing."

This leads the logical among us to conclude that it is not our decision to accept Christ that makes us acceptable to Christ. If it was, then we would have to say that salvation comes by putting sin on hold long enough to make a righteous decision. But Romans 3:10 says no one can do that, for "not one is righteous, no, not one." Scripture also says (Romans 5:8) that Christ died for our sakes while we were still sinners. Since one of the many sins of sinners is that of rejecting Christ, the startling truth is that Christ saves while people are rejecting Him, not while they are accepting Him.

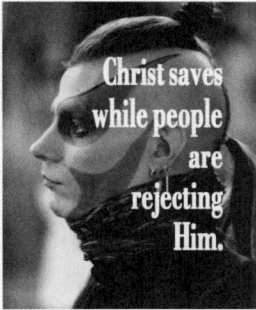

Christ saves while people are rejecting Him.

Turn back to page 39. In the picture on the right, you are looking at Edmund just before I told him the good news that Jesus Christ already saved and justified him two thousand years ago. This surprised the heck out of him. Edmund said the pastor at his old church had told him that, in order to be saved and justified, he had to at least put sin on hold long enough to make a wise decision. This only made him drink and smoke more, he said, because he felt so unable to do that. Upon hearing the good news that, in spite of his drinking and smoking, Christ saved and justified him two thousand years ago, Edmund believed it. He then got up out of his chair, took a shower, made some coffee, and told me that, since he was already saved and justified, (and had come to believe it by the grace of God), he may as well start acting like it.

Romans 5:20—"Where sin increases, grace superexceeds"

Where did *that* verse come from? Answer: from the pen of an inspired sinner—Paul.

You can't out-sin grace. Romans 5:20 is not a misprint. You can sin and sin and sin, and still not blow your salvation. In fact, sinning and sinning and sinning only invites grace, grace, and more grace. If it wasn't your behavior that got you into Christ (which is the clear testimony of 2 Timothy 1:9), then how can it be your behavior that gets you out?

You've never heard this in church because your church doesn't believe it. Your church assumes that the kind of freedom we're uncovering here—even if they did believe it—will inspire more sin. Christian leaders don't trust grace, and they certainly don't trust you with it. So they prop up grace with law, make themselves the administrators of it, and send you on a guilt trip every time you miss church or break one of their rules. But as we just saw with Edmund, appreciating grace makes you sin less because you're so thankful to discover how free you are. It's a beautiful paradox. Hearing from the clergy that they must stop sinning at least long enough to earn their "free grace" is what drives honest people like Edmund to liquor cabinets. The truth doesn't do that. The truth makes people want to drink orange juice and praise Jesus for doing what they could not possibly do.

All is allowed me

Paul said in 1 Corinthians 6:12, "All is allowed me, but not all is expedient." Ever heard *this* truth in church?

Probably not. But I'll bet you've heard this:

Pastor Ken: All is allowed you.
Congregation: (together) *Really?*
Pastor Ken: Yes, and here's a list of those things, drafted by elder Bill and myself...

Allowing yourself the freedom to do anything is the only way to curb your flesh. I know it's a paradox, but it's nevertheless true. It is also true that "not all is expedient." In other words, eating six Big Macs a day won't imperil your salvation (grace will rise to the occasion and overwhelm you), but you'll probably die of heart failure before the end of the month.

Twist and shout

People will twist my words, I know, because there are people in this world who make a living downgrading grace to allow for works. Here's how they'll do it: "Martin Zender says that we should go out and sin more, so that more grace will come. We should go and kick canes out from old ladies."

Well, I just word-searched this document and couldn't find either "canes," "kick," or "old ladies." Some of these elderly women are very good with their ambulatory props, and they will give you something, somewhere, to remember them by. I never said any of this.

This sin/grace argument is nothing new. Paul anticipated it way back when. After laying out the radical truth of Romans 5:20, Paul quickly adds in 6:1-2: "What, then, shall we declare? That we may be persisting in sin that grace should be increasing? May it not be coming to that!"

This argument had already surfaced in Romans 3:5 and Romans 3:8. It comes up again in Romans 6:15. Paul doesn't condemn the hypothetical question (the question is proof that his shocking point has hit home), he condemns an affirmative answer *to* the question. The fact that these arguments are even raised proves that the hypothetical arguers have at least grasped Paul's message. That's more than can be said of people today.

"I guarantee that you can screw up grace. Grace isn't what you think it is. Jesus didn't mean to let you off the hook. I can pretty much guarantee that you're eventually going to do something really, really sinful and send yourself to hell."

No one grasps Paul's message today because no one hears it. What congregant stands up in church today and says, "Are you implying, Pastor, that we should sin more so that more grace will come?" The pastor's message doesn't invite this objection because his message is not one of radical grace. What his message does invite is, "Which sins must I avoid, Pastor, in order to be right with God?" Or, "Which sins have I already committed, Pastor, that have ruined God's opinion of me?" Professional pastors neither preach on nor even quote Romans 5:20; in fact, they banish it to the outer darkness where it weeps and gnashes its teeth.

Where Paul's radical teachings of grace go unspoken, there are no misunderstandings. Where grace's astounding power is never announced, the astounding question of Romans 6:1 never arises. That *I* field this question for a living assures me that I'm teaching Paul correctly, and that my grace message is as true and startling today as it was two thousand years ago.

RENEWING THE MIND

"For by faith are we walking, not by perception."
—*the Apostle Paul,* 2 Corinthians 5:7

Objective truth

Have you ever heard of objective truth? Objective truth doesn't care what you think about it. That's a Martin Zender definition. Random House defines objective this way: "not affected by personal feelings or prejudice; based on facts; unbiased." Like I said, objective truth doesn't care what you think about it.

How do you feel, personally, about the sun rising every morning? Does it trouble you? Excite you? Does it make you want to scramble eggs—or roll over in bed? The sun doesn't care about your opinion; it comes up no matter what you think of it. The sun brightening the earth every morning is objective truth. You can like it, you can hate it, you can pull the shades on it or let it into your bedroom. Either way, here comes the sun.

The things I told you in the previous section are objective truths. These are things that Christ has already done for you whether you enjoy them or not. You may not be able to see or feel them, but they're no less real.

Freedom from sin is one of these truths. Freedom from sin is a done deal. It was accomplished two thousand years ago at Calvary. Now that you've seen how all mankind is wrapped up in the work of two, you can better understand how freedom from sin thrives independently of your walk. It focuses only on what Christ did on the cross. The happy result is that you are free from the guilt, condemnation and discouragement that normally follow in the wake of failure.

Freed from sin

Romans 8:2- "The spirit's law of life in Christ Jesus frees you from the law of sin and death."

Romans 6:18- "Now, being freed from Sin, you are enslaved to Righteousness."

Romans 6:11- "Thus you also, be reckoning yourselves to be dead, indeed, to Sin, yet living to God in Christ Jesus, our Lord."

That's funny. I don't feel like I'm free from sin. But so it is with objective truth. Objective truth is based on fact, not feeling. This is why Paul speaks in **2 Corinthians**

5:7 of walking by faith, not perception. Let this verse anchor you throughout this section.

In the three verses quoted above, the first two are facts, and the third is a strong recommendation based on the facts. Here are your options: You can either believe the facts (walk by faith) and enjoy the third verse while smoking a cigarette, or you can concentrate on the cigarette (walk by perception), kick yourself for being such a sinner, and ignore all three verses.

Concerning Romans 6:11, reckoning yourself to be dead, indeed, to Sin, has nothing to do with how much or how little you sin. You can be dead to Sin and still be a sinner. How? Being dead to Sin (I capitalize it here to personify it) means that you are dead to its accusations that God is still mad at you. You don't listen to it telling you how guilty and condemned you are. Why? Because you're not. Being dead to Sin is like being dead to the world. You're in the world, but not of it; you don't hear its voices. Being dead to Sin doesn't mean you no longer sin. You just no longer pay attention to Sin's snide remarks.

I have two very important things to tell you now concerning deliverance from sin. These require a walk of faith, not perception. These two simple statements will change your life and put deliverance ministries out of business:

- Deliverance from Sin comes, not through victory over it, but through death to it.
- Deliverance from Sin doesn't change the sin, it changes your attitude *toward* the sin.

My apologies to the deliverance ministries.

A slave of subjectivity

In my excitement over these objective passages, I forgot to give you the definition of subjective. Here's how Random House sees it: "placing emphasis or reliance on one's own moods, attitudes, opinions, etc." Subjectivity, therefore, requires walking by perception.

Abraham Lincoln freed the slaves nearly 143 years ago. This is objective, historical truth. It's something Abraham Lincoln *did*. Is there one African American alive today still claiming to be a slave? There must not be, because Barbara Walters would have interviewed him or her by now. But let's say there was one.

Walters: So, Mr. Williamson, you actually believe you're still a slave?

Williamson: Sure do, Miss Barbara.

Walters: But Abraham Lincoln freed the slaves 143

years ago.

Williamson: So they say, Miss Barbara. But I'm into this subjective thing.

Walters: Can you enlarge upon that, Mr. Williamson?

Williamson: Sure. I still *feel* like a slave. I'm, like, in this slave *mood*. Are you following me?

Walters: Yes, I understand subjectivity. It seems to me that you're walking by perception—*your* perception.

Williamson: I guess you could say it like that.

Walters: But don't you think that objective truth overrules that? Where's your faith in the Emancipation Proclamation?

Williamson: Yes, well, where *is* the Emancipation Proclamation?

Walters: It's true that the original document was lost in the Chicago Fire, but I don't see how that should have any bearing on this.

Williamson: Yes, well, I'm just not an objective type person, Miss Barbara. You *say* Mister Abraham wrote such a thing so many years ago, but I don't see it. And even if

I did see it, I don't know that I'd believe it. You may say, "this is objective truth," but objective things are too hard to understand. I hang on my moods and feelings. They're easier for me.

Walters: But isn't this causing you a lot of trouble? I mean, here we are hiding under hay bales in a barn outside Ripley, Ohio. You call this easy?

Williamson: Yes, well, this is better accommodations than what they had at the Vinson place down in Drip Rock.

Walters: Mr. Williamson, what are your goals for the future?

Williamson: One goal, Miss Barbara. Freedom. I'm looking to be in Canada by week's end.

Walters: Are you sure you don't want to think more on what Abraham Lincoln did back there in 1863? I'm asking you this as a friend. Can't you simply believe that President Lincoln signed your freedom into law and that this law serves you today?

Williamson: Now, don't you confuse me, Miss Barbara. I got my subjective course lined up for the next several days. I don't need nobody confusing me with their objective ideology.

Walters: Well, good luck, Mr. Williamson. And if you see Miss Tubman...

Williamson: I'll tell her you said, "hey."

———————

An absurd interview? Yes. But no more absurd than a person freed from sin two thousand years ago still fighting to be free from sin. Does this person *feel* guilty? Does it *seem* to him or her that God's condemnation still reigns? Objective truth may be harder to grasp than the subjective world that sits atop one's nose, but it's worth trying for. It's the difference between walking by faith and walking by perception. It's the difference between happiness and guilt.

Freed from sin while infirm in the flesh

Romans 6:18-19: "Now, being freed from Sin, you are enslaved to Righteousness. As a man am I saying this, because of the infirmity of your flesh."

The apostle Paul slipped a truth in there so slick-like that many miss it. Did you see how Paul pronounced the Romans freed from sin and infirm in the flesh at the same time? Religion has told you that these things are mutually exclusive. But no. This is the result of understanding that objective truth (faith) overrules subjective opinion (perception).

Someone deposited one million dollars in your bank account Thursday. But nobody told you about it. So today, you're still fretting over the electric bill, still troubled by your rumbling muffler, still wearing worn-out clothes. The truth—the objective truth—is that you

are rich. You living like a down-and-outer does not affect the fact of your wealth. The fact of your wealth is
objective truth. Your ignorance is chaining you to what
your senses perceive. You're a subjective peasant living
in an objective mansion.

In the Williamson interview, Ms. Walters tried to
emphasize something that Abraham Lincoln *did*. As
human experience cannot alter historical fact, Ms.
Walters did the right thing. Let me quote Romans 8:2
again, only this time I'll follow it with verse 3:

> For the spirit's law of life in Christ Jesus frees
> you from the law of sin and death. For what was
> impossible to the law, in which it was infirm through
> the flesh, did God, sending His own Son in the like-
> ness of sin's flesh and concerning sin, He condemns
> sin in the flesh.

The most important words of this text, besides
"Christ Jesus frees you from the law of sin and death"
are the words "DID GOD." I have these two words
circled so many time in my Bible that the impression
from my pen shows through three pages. Freedom from
sin is something *God did*. Period. Done. Signed, sealed,
delivered.

Before leaving this section, notice how Paul starts
out with, "*Now*, being freed from Sin..." This is what

I've been saying. The Romans were freed from Sin *then*. And so are you today. It was a done deal then, it's a done deal now. It was an objective truth then, and it's the same today. The result of this, Paul says, is that the Romans are "enslaved to Righteousness." Note: they *are* enslaved to Righteousness. Does this mean that none of the Romans smoked? No. "Enslaved to Righteousness" means that Jesus Christ now owned them, rather than Sin. Nothing has yet changed with the Romans, they just switched hands. First, they were enslaved to Sin, and now they're enslaved to Righteousness, all as a result of what God did.

Drum roll, please...

Romans 8:10 seems so anticlimactic: "Now if Christ is in you, the body, indeed, is dead because of sin, yet the spirit is life because of righteousness."

Those words, "Now if Christ is in you..." sound like a drum roll. The words are so full of fanfare that you expect something wonderful to follow, something like, "If Christ is in you...you begin to achieve all your godly goals." Or, "If Christ is in you...you command morality until the day you die." Or, "If Christ is in you...sin is but a distant memory."

But no. What does the verse really say? "Now if Christ is in you, *the body, indeed, is dead because of sin...*"

"Your breath still stinks."

If Christ is in you, the body remains flesh. If your breath was bad before Christ, it will be bad after. The spirit will not, this side of immortality, transform a body of humiliation into a body of glory. It's true that the influence of Christ will cause a body of humiliation to, say, bake cookies for a sick neighbor. This is where the second part of the verse comes in, "yet the spirit is life because of righteousness." But the important thing to note here is that spirit is spirit and flesh is flesh. Spirit will inspire flesh, but it will not transform it this side of immortality.

Now you see the real thrill of the verse. The presence of Christ in your life is not your signal to perform. The presence of Christ in your life puts the spirit to work, not you.

I'll never forget how wonderful it felt when I learned that I didn't have to live like Jesus Christ. It set me at perfect peace to learn, rather, that Jesus Christ was supposed to live His life through me.

"Stay High, Sweet Chariot"

Why are so many people afraid of Christ? It's because they're under the misconception (engendered by troublesome Christians) that a walk with Christ means giving up bad (but fun) habits. This was Edmund's problem in the last chapter. Surprisingly, it was Edmund's church that turned him against God. Like apostate Israel of old, orthodox Christianity is God's worst public relations nightmare. They inadvertently defame His name among thinking people everywhere, attributing to Him such hideous traits and hanging on Him such asinine doctrines (doctrines such as, "I'll love you unconditionally as long as you love Me") that not even the most calloused unbeliever could concoct them, let alone believe them.

Edmund's pastor told him he had to become a non-sinner at least long enough to make a wise decision and accept Christ, and if he didn't he'd be hell-bound. Since Edmund didn't feel he had this kind of righteousness in him (he was the only honest person in the church, for "not one is righteous, no, not one," Romans 3:10) the pastor's message discouraged him and caused him to drink more. Not until I told Edmund that Christ had already justified him did Edmund become joyful enough (this was the work of the spirit within him) to want to live a better life.

Edmund saw through the hypocrisy of those who claimed to have a message of grace, but then told him that he had to "reach for it." He was saved by grace, the pastor assured him, but unless he "accepted Jesus," Jesus would not accept him. *Strange brand of grace*, thought Edmund, knocking back another swig of Jack Daniels. I told Edmund that Jesus Christ had already accepted him even while he was a sinner. Finally seeing salvation as a fact rather than a challenge, Edmund believed what Christ did for him and desired to live for the One Who had delivered him from sin and death.

I do feel sorry for unbelievers—or for anyone, really—who think that orthodox Christian meetings, services, Bible studies and the like will ease their burdens. It is there that their burdens will multiply. First, they will learn that they must "make a wise decision to believe in Jesus" or else Jesus will have no choice but to hand them over to be tortured for eternity. This, of course, will be called "the good news." Then they will be told that they must show God how thankful they are to have escaped this eternal torture by

"I go to church so that Jesus won't torture me."

giving up their bad habits, by loving people unconditionally, by being baptized, and by going to church regu-
larly. If they fail to do these things, they will be told that
it's possible they were never really saved in the first place,
and Jesus will probably end up having to torture them
anyway.

Whee-ha. What a message. What a gospel.

Chicken bodies

If Christ is in you, the body is indeed dead, yet the
spirit is life (Romans 8:10). In other words, your spirit
soars long before your body figures out what's going on.
If you're expecting your body to keep up with your revelations, you're setting yourself up for discouragement.
Believers who continually monitor their bodies are
deeply unhappy people. The remedy? **Romans 6:6**—

> Knowing this, that our old humanity was
> crucified together with Him, that the body of Sin may
> be nullified.

The truth of our crucifixion with Christ soothes us
long before our flesh obeys us. Read the verse again: our
old humanity was crucified (done deal), that the body
of sin may be nullified (future expectation). Thus, we
ought not panic when our bodies lag behind our revela-

tions. It will always be this way until the day Christ changes us. Yes, we groan for this to happen—read Romans 8:23—as we await the deliverance of our bodies; our bodies drive us crazy sometimes. But we should not groan to the point of discouragement and frustration. We want the change, of course, but we shouldn't rush God's timing.

Have you ever seen a chicken with its head cut off? I never have, thank God. But people in the know tell me that when you cut a chicken's head off, the chicken continues running around the farm until its body catches up with what just happened to it.

Weird.

Christ delivered a deathblow to sin. Because of His work on the cross, sin can no longer condemn us. The tricky part about this is that this truth is much smarter than our bodies. Our freedom from sin is won long before we stop sinning. Like the chicken's sprinting frame, our bodies are slow to realize what has been accomplished in the spiritual realm. It's hard to convince ourselves we're free from sin when our bodies are touring the barnyard.

This is where walking by faith comes in. Can our spirits soar with Christ even while our bodies are slopping at the trough? Yes—if we walk by faith, not perception. This kind of walk inspired Paul's remarkable recommendation in Romans 6:13—"Present yourselves to God as if alive from among the dead."

Does Paul actually mean that we're to *pretend* to be alive from among the dead? This is certainly the sense of "as if." It's a walk of faith. Well, look at yourself. How could it be anything but?

Scratching air

Another example from nature will illustrate this truth. Have you ever heard of phantom limb pain? Phantom limb pain is a physiological phenomenon that plagues amputees. A man who has had his leg removed, for instance, will continue to feel pain in the "leg" long after it's gone. He will even feel tickling sensations in the "leg," and will often reach down to scratch it.

Margaret: Billy, what are you doing?
Billy: What does it look like I'm doing?
Margaret: It looks like you're waving at my carpet.
Billy: Well I'm not. I'm scratching my right leg.
Margaret: But, Billy. You don't *have* a right leg.
Billy: Mind your own business, Margaret, and get me a stool for this thing.

Six months ago, my wife's grandfather had his toes amputated. Recently, we asked him how he was feeling.
"My toes hurt!" he said.
It was phantom limb pain.

The mind knows that the body part is gone, but the body still sends signals that the part hurts or itches. Thus also with freedom from sin. Sometimes you just have to accept the facts while watching yourself smoke a cigarette.

Living in faith

Galatians 2:20: "With Christ have I been crucified, yet I am living; no longer I, but living in me is Christ. Now that which I am now living in flesh, I am living in faith that is of the Son of God, Who loves me, and gives Himself up for me."

Paul recognized that he had been crucified with Christ. But wasn't Paul still alive? Yes. "Crucified with Christ" is a figure of speech for being so identified with Christ in His death that you're no longer wrapped up in what you do, but in what He did. You now see Him instead of yourself. What a happy place to be. Paul had applied the truths of Calvary so thoroughly that he saw himself as having died and been resurrected with Christ. This is a bold walk of faith that operates in spite of our failing frames. Yes, even Paul possessed a failing frame, for see how he finishes: "That which I am now living in flesh, I am living in faith."

Faith denies evidence. Paul's body wasn't perfect, and Paul knew it. Did it trouble him? On occasion, yes, just as our bodies trouble us. Paul's body was busy trying to talk him out of truths that his intellect had long accepted: "*You? Justified?* You're living in a fantasy world, Paul. Look at me. Look at your body." But Paul refused to do it. The life that Paul still lived in the flesh, he lived in faith. Faith is the only solution to a body that refuses to accept a revelation.

We do Paul a disservice to put him in stained glass. The word faith here tells us that Paul accepted something as fact that he couldn't detect with his senses. Had this not been the case, where would faith come in? That Paul's flesh life was a matter for faith to remedy proves that Paul still sinned. A flawless Paul would have no need for faith. But Paul's body, like yours and mine, still humiliated him, still mocked his revelation. This is why he said in 2 Corinthians 5:7, "By faith are we walking, not perception."

Are you walking by perception? No wonder you're miserable.

Think: I'm freed from sin (Romans 6:18).

Walk: as if alive from among the dead (Romans 6:13).

See: yourself as God sees you (Romans. 5:10).

Set your mind: on what Christ has done, not on what you are doing (Romans 5:8).

THINK. WALK. SEE. SET.

The case of the exasperated apostle

In Romans, chapter 7, we behold an exasperated man—it's the apostle Paul again. Listen to his complaint in verses 18 through 24, and tell me if you've been here:

> For I am aware that good is not making its home in me (that is, in my flesh), for to will is lying beside me, yet to be effecting the ideal is not. For it is not the good that I will that I am doing, but the evil that I am not willing, *this* I am putting into practice. Now if what I am not willing, this I am doing, it is no longer I who am effecting it, but Sin which is making its home in me. Consequently, I am finding the law that, at my willing to be doing the ideal, the evil is lying beside me. For I am gratified with the law of God as to the man within, yet I am observing a different law in my members, warring with the law of my mind, and leading me into captivity to the law of sin which is in my members. A wretched man am I! What will rescue me out of this body of death? Grace!

Feel the pain; we've all experienced it. We want to do right, but we can't. We will to do good, but we end up doing evil. We love God and want so much to please Him—or do we? There's something going on in our flesh that batters our will. It taunts the will and mocks it, making us do the opposite of what we want. What a mess we're in. No, it's a flat-out war.

Paul says that he is gratified with the law of God as to the man within. The spirit in Paul says, "This is the ideal!" Our spirits say the same thing. Give yourself credit for it. "Yet," Paul says, "I am observing a different law in my members, warring with the law of my mind, and leading me into captivity to the law of sin which is in my members. A wretched man am I! What will rescue me out of this body of death?"

Like us, Paul despairs that his body lags so far behind his revelation. His mind grasps the truth—he understands that he has been freed from sin—but his body won't adjust to it. What will rescue Paul out of his body of death? The answer: Grace.

That the answer to Paul's dilemma is grace proves that his body has not changed. Grace is favor granted to those deserving the opposite. If God's answer to Paul's problem was, "Here's a sinless body," grace would not apply. There can be no grace apart from sin. Sin is the petri dish where grace flourishes. Take away the petri dish (the sin), and grace cannot exist. Without sin, there are no unworthies on whom to lavish it. But there is more evidence still that Paul remained a sinner.

I have quoted this passage down to verse 24. Now I'm going to quote verse 25. Don't drop your lighter.

Verse 25: "I thank God, through Jesus Christ, our

Lord. Consequently, then, I myself, with the mind, indeed, am slaving for God's law, yet with the flesh for Sin's law."

What has changed with Paul's body since he has come to this marvelous recognition of God's grace? Nothing. The word "consequently" introduces the result of all that Paul has been considering. I've heard many commentators say that the seventh chapter of Romans is Paul putting himself in the place of a man who still sins. "Paul isn't really like this anymore," the commentators say. "That was the old Paul. That was the Pharisee Saul, before he became Paul. The new Paul doesn't sin anymore. The new Paul would never think the way the Paul of Romans 7:18-24 thought." If these commentators are right, then verse 25 should read like this:

"Consequently, then (the result of all this is), I, myself am no longer sinning."

Or like this: "Consequently, then, I can all of a sudden do everything I want to do."

Or like this: "Consequently, then, evil is no longer lying beside me, and I can now resist every temptation."

But the commentators are wrong, because Romans 7:25 reads this way:

"Consequently, then, I myself, with the mind, indeed, am slaving for God's law, yet with the flesh for Sin's law."

Even after realizing the grace of God, Paul is still slav-

ing for Sin's law with his flesh.

If Paul's flesh hasn't changed, then what has? This: Paul has been delivered from the war with his flesh.

Glory! Freedom! Deliverance!

Paul said in verse 23, "I am observing a different law in my members, warring with the law of my mind, and leading me into captivity."

It was not his flesh, but the *war* with his flesh that was leading Paul into captivity. It's the same with you and me. Are we warring with our flesh? Then we are miserable, for this is captivity. To be constantly worrying about, wrestling against, and warring with the flesh is the worst kind of bondage. So many people assume that a vast moral struggle must accompany a Christian walk. Christianity itself has taught this. But no. This is horrible bondage. Struggling against flesh is the essence

"I'm sick of all the worldly people not being miserable!"

of religion and it's why religion frustrates people and makes them crazy. It's why religious people become incensed that the rest of the world isn't as concerned with sin as they are. The truth is that the rest of the world trusts God more with its sin than Christians do with theirs.

- *Grace delivers us, not from our flesh, but from the war with our flesh.*
- *Deliverance from sin comes, not through victory over it, but through death to it.*
- *Deliverance from sin doesn't change the sin, it changes our attitude toward the sin.*

The war is over

2 Corinthians 10:3-5:

> For, walking in flesh, we are not warring according to the flesh. For the weapons of our warfare are not fleshly, but powerful to God toward the pulling down of bulwarks; pulling down reckonings and every height elevating itself against the knowledge of God, and leading into captivity every apprehension into the obedience of Christ.

The only effective remedy for flesh is to ignore it and to focus on God. By taking our focus off of ourselves and sending it Godward, we will pull down the bulwark of sin that elevates itself against the knowledge of God. And there's the paradox. By not focusing on self, self will begin conforming to Christ.

The result for Paul was a glad one, causing him to say in 2 Corinthians 4:16: "Wherefore we are not despondent, but even if our outward man is decaying, nevertheless that within us is being renewed day by day."

Paul learned to segregate flesh from spirit. He learned that, even while the outward man is decaying, that within is being renewed. Here in Romans, chapter 7, Paul has given up on his body. This confirms his statement in Galatians, that the life he lived in flesh was one of faith. How humiliating this must have been, whenever Paul faced religious people. The outward man was the man that showed. It was the man that did not always complement Paul's spiritual vision. Even so, Paul was not despondent. The grace of God had rescued him from that.

Should auld acquaintance be forgot? Definitely.

2 Corinthians 5:16- "So that we, from now on, are acquainted with no one according to flesh. Yet even if we have known Christ according to flesh, nevertheless now we know Him so no longer."

I believe that being acquainted with no one according to flesh includes ourselves. There comes a time in the life of a believer when he or she is to stop thinking of the Savior as the dusty Nazarene and consider Him as He is now, glorified at the right hand of God. This accompanies progression toward maturity. Likewise, mature believers also come to stop considering themselves after the flesh, and concentrate instead on how God sees them: justified in Christ, flawless in His sight. Let's graduate from immaturity to maturity. Let's graduate from putting our lives up on graphs and monitoring our progress toward perfection. Instead, let's walk by faith and focus on what Christ has done for our spirits.

What is a slave of Sin?

We know now what it is to be free from sin. What is it, then, to be a slave of Sin? Keep in mind that, whenever we speak of slavery to Sin, we speak subjectively, not objectively.

Romans 6:17- "Now...you were slaves of Sin..."

Most people think that a slave of Sin is someone who sins. But this is not the whole truth. A slave of Sin is just as much someone who fights his or her sin as someone who indulges it. The issue is: Sin. Do you fret about your sin? Then you're a slave of Sin. Are you worried that your sin is removing you from God's favor? Then you're a slave of Sin. Are you trying to remove sin from your life? Then you're a slave of Sin. It doesn't matter if you're sinning like crazy or trying like crazy not to sin. This issue is sin, and in both cases, apart from God's revelation, you're a slave of it. Here's how it works:

Slave of sin   Slave of sin

Any questions so far? Good.

The measure to which you sin has no effect on whether you are either free from Sin or a slave of it. You can be free from Sin while sinning, and you can be a slave of Sin while refraining from it. How can this be? In the first case, you are appreciating what Christ has done for you at Calvary, even while smoking a cigarette. Smoking cigarettes will give you lung cancer, that's true, but it can never separate you from the love of God and Christ, Who freed you from the law of sin and death. Are you feeling good in Christ, even while you're smoking? Then you're subjectively confirming an objective truth. Not that evidence is necessary, but feeling good in spite of your sin is proof that you're free from it. It's a subjective confirmation of an objective truth, reflected in your happy walk. In the second case (being a slave of Sin while refraining from it), you have donned your holy attire, knelt in a quiet place, and have strained to produce a sinless five minutes. Did it feel good? No. The pressure just about killed you. So you're a slave of Sin.

Romans 4:8- "Happy the man to whom the Lord by no means should be reckoning sin!"

Philippians 4:6- "Don't worry about anything."

Don't worry, be happy. Perhaps you didn't realize that this was scriptural advice.

STARVING NEGATIVITY

Passions and Lusts

"Now those of Christ Jesus crucify the flesh together with its passions and lusts" (Galatians 5:24).

If there are any rapists, child molesters or drug dealers reading, hello and welcome. I'm sorry I haven't acknowledged you until now. Everything in this book applies to you, just as it applies to the person who smokes, overeats, or covets his neighbor's wife. For the sake of everyone's good, however, I am hoping you are reading this in jail. If you're not, then may someone haul your dangerous ass in. Got a sentence? Good. Now use your time wisely and read and re-read this book. Imbibe of Paul's gospel of grace (read Romans), and God's unconditional love for you. Grace is grace, and God now sees you through His Son. There is now, therefore, no condemnation! (This is God's viewpoint, not the court's.) Having said this, I would like to invite you—and everyone—to now consider your milder passions and lusts, those troublesome things we often call bad habits.

I welcome the passionate and lustful, then, to paragraph two. Everybody okay with crucifixion? Hm. Perhaps not. Perhaps you're not sure whether you want all your passions and lusts crucified; this may get ugly. If this is you, proceed to the next paragraph.

I appreciate your honesty. Some passions and lusts are so near and dear to us that we wonder how we could live without them. No more shopping sprees? Lord, take me now. If you're having second thoughts about giving up your passions and lusts, continue to paragraph four.

Hi, and welcome to paragraph four. Sometimes it's unwise to manhandle our errant desires. Besides, if we stopped drinking two pots of coffee a day or lusting after the opposite sex, we might start beating the children. This is why the apostle Paul recommends crucifixion, rather than a direct attack, for passions and lusts. Intrigued? Please continue.

We often think that crucifying passions and lusts means attacking and destroying them. But how would that encourage a life of freedom and peace in Christ? Christ frees us for freedom (Galatians 5:1) and for peace

(Ephesians 2:17). How can people who are wrestling their flesh all day feel free and peaceful? Is it possible that crucifying passions and lusts means something other than turning our Christian faith into a test of willpower? If you answered, "God, I hope so," then continue to the next paragraph.

Congratulations on being honest enough to have made it this far. Here, we will learn what the apostle Paul had in mind when he wrote, "Crucify your passions and lusts."

I remind you that crucifixion was unlike ordinary execution in that the victim did not die by direct violence (e.g., firing squad, hanging, drowning, beheading, etc.) but by deprivational violence. By this I mean that crucifixion deprived its victims of vital, life-sustaining elements such as oxygen, food and water. Crucifixion itself never killed anybody. What killed a person was either the asphyxiation, hunger, or thirst that resulted from being unable to either draw a decent breath, get to a well for water, or visit the commissary. Many victims of crucifixion—sorry to relate—lasted several days on the cross. If you are eager to understand how this applies to M&Ms, Macy's and *Maxim* magazine, please continue.

Here is where I help you understand how deprivational death, rather than violent attack, is the best way to manage passions and lusts.

It is a well-known, natural phenomenon—not un-like gravity—that the more we human beings concentrate on trying not to do something, the more likely we are to do it. As this principle is as immutable as gravity, the human being who feels guilty about it might just as well feel that way about falling down instead of up. If it would comfort anyone to learn that even a man of God had problems with his inability to do the good he really wanted to do, then we will forge on to paragraph twelve.

The apostle Paul once confessed to some friends in Rome:

> I should never have felt guilty of the sin of covet-ing if I had not heard the law saying, 'Thou shalt not covet.' But the sin in me, finding in the com-mandment an opportunity to express itself, stimu-lated all my desires (Romans 7:7-8) I know from experience that the carnal side of my being can scarcely be called the home of good! I often find that I have the will to do good, but not the power. That is, I don't accomplish the good I set out to do, and the evil I don't really want to do I find I am always doing (Romans 7: 18-19).

If this is you, go to the next paragraph.

Looks like we coaxed quite a few people into para-graph fourteen. If those in front would kindly move up, those standing outside may at least get in the door. For

Paul, there was only one way out of his dilemma: "What will rescue me out of this body of death? Grace!" (Romans 7:24, Concordant Literal New Testament). For a quick lesson on grace, please continue.

As I pointed out earlier, grace cannot function without sin any more than forgiveness can function without offense. If we quit sinning (not that we could if we tried), God would have nothing to be gracious toward us about. If the answer to Paul's dilemma was "grace," it logically follows that Paul still sinned, even after writing this confession. If Paul had stopped sinning, what need would there have been for grace? If the answer to you having to wait for Christmas is "patience," does Christmas arrive? No. The fact that the answer is patience proves that Christmas has not arrived. No one needs patience to await something that has come. Grace is a gift given to those deserving the opposite. If people start deserving grace, they no longer need it. If grace is the answer to passions and lusts, then a few of these irritants must remain, whether we like them or not. If you're wondering now whether this means that you can sin and enjoy grace at the same time—keep reading.

Of course you can. You can't enjoy grace *unless* you sin.

Well, now I've done it. Here comes the standard objection—again: "What, then, shall we declare? That we may be persisting in sin that grace should be increasing?" (Romans 6:1). And this: "What, then? Should we be sinning, seeing that we are not under law, but under grace?" (Romans 6:15). I might just as well ask: If my wife has promised to excuse me every time I burp, should I drink nine bottles of ginger ale and belch in her ear? That would be rude. But since my wife has promised to excuse me every time I burp, I could certainly do it if I wanted to. That's the thing. Christ promises through Paul in Romans 5:20: "Where sin increases, grace superexceeds." You can theologize around that all you want, but it's an immutable law. More water does not drown a ship; it only causes it to

float higher. But this analogy falls short because the ship rises in proportion to the rising water. With sin and grace, grace superexceeds the sin; it's disproportional; the grace is undeserved. To approach it in the ship example, I might have to say something like: the more water you remove from the ocean, the higher the ship floats. It's that shocking, and that strange. It's that wonderful.

It's grace.

While Paul would deter us from proving the sin/ grace law for the sport of it, the principle remains. Because I believe that Romans 5:20 is literal and immutable, I can boldly say that, while I don't recommend testing grace, you could certainly do it and get away with it because grace is more than equal to anything you could possibly do.

Now, finally, for the secret of how to crucify passions and lusts and still remain imperfect enough to enjoy grace, please read on.

Passions and lusts are always rising up, trying to make us feel like bad Christians who either better shape up or roast like chestnuts on an eternal fire. That just goes to show how ignorant passions and lusts are; they don't realize that grace depends on their existence. We discussed earlier how that the more human beings try not to do something, the more they do it. Don't you think our passions and lusts know that? That's why they are always rising up to challenge us; they want to get us so mad at them that we will try hard not to do them. This, of course, delights them, because, as many fallen ministers and the apostle Paul himself ably demonstrated, trying not to do them makes us do them even more. What a victory for the passions and lusts. Are you beginning to see what Paul meant when he said that we ought to administer to these moral irritants a deprivational death rather than a violent attack? A violent attack is only a temporary scare fix, while a deprivational death starves passions and lusts from the inside out. If you are beginning to see this, then by all means continue.

Remember how the crucified died, their bodies starved of essential, life-giving elements? Do that to your passions and lusts. Instead of trying to shoot them, or hang them, or behead them, simply ignore them. I know that doesn't sound like very Biblical advice, but it is. Jesus Himself offered it when He said, "If, then, your eye should be single, your whole body will be luminous"

The Dietary Trials of Ann

"Just stop thinking about double-dipped chocolate-covered peanuts. Double-dipped chocolate-covered peanuts are bad. Forget totally about double-dipped chocolate-covered peanuts. *Ann? Are you listening to me?*"

(Matthew 6:22). Never mind the body, Jesus said. Keep your eye on Me, and the body will take care of itself.

In 1 Corinthians 9:27, Paul says he belabors his body: "Now then, thus am I racing, not as dubious, thus am I boxing, not as punching the air, but I am belaboring my body and leading it into slavery." Was Paul on a self-help program to improve his flesh? Does this verse cancel all previous truth from Paul's pen? No, it confirms it.

The Greek word translated "belabor" here is *hupopiazo*. The elements are UNDER-VIEWIZE; *hupo* means "under," and *piazo* has to do with "the viewer," that is, the eye. The meaning of the word, according to page 28 of the Greek-English Keyword Concordance to the Concordant Literal New Testament is, "to blacken by a blow that part of the face which is under the eye." Marvelous! Does Paul flail at his body with inconsequential blows? No, not him.

Paul uses several sports analogies in his writings. Apparently, he knew a thing or two about boxing. Paul knew that any boxer wishing to quickly end a fight would go for his opponent's eye. What do boxers protect the most? They protect their faces, especially their eyes. What Paul is saying here is that, in order to bring his entire body under subjection to Christ, he needs to subject only one part, and that is the eye. It confirms the truth our Lord spoke: "If, then, your eye should be single, your whole body will be luminous." This is all figurative, of course; Paul is not literally jabbing himself in the cornea, and neither is Jesus speaking of literal light. What Paul is doing is focusing his attention—his spiritual eye—upon Christ.

If someone asked you to contract your pupil, how would you do it? Would you get your grimy fingers in there and try to squish the delicate organ into shape? Why do that when you can simply lift up your head and look at the sun? Likewise: How would you conform your body to the image of Christ? Works?

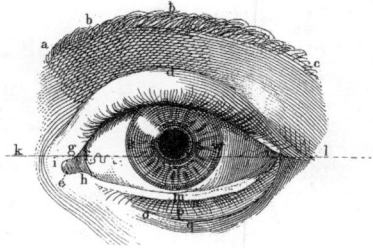

Willpower? A longer flagellum? Why do that when you can simply lift up your head and look at the Son?

When a farmer wants to plant a straight furrow, what does he do? Ask any farmer, and he'll tell you. First of all, he does not look at the furrow. He looks at a point—such as a tree—on the distant horizon. It's a paradox. A farmer plants a straight furrow by ignoring the furrow.

When you crucify a passion or a lust it means that whenever the thing raises its ugly head, instead of fighting it, you ignore it. Mind you, this passion or lust is not mere temptation, but a manifested thing, that is, it is something that has already happened. Paul is not telling us here how to avoid sin, but rather how to deal with it once it has manifested itself. Are you keeping a thankful eye to Christ and His grace? Then the thing will take care of itself. Eventually. My advice is: Get out of the way and let grace do its strange work. This requires a radical, childlike trust in God.

Passions and lusts require your attention to survive, especially the attention required to try to fix them. Rob them of this, and they will starve to death. Some may still be supposing that this merely means we must resist temptation. If this is you, please go to the next paragraph.

What have I been saying? For one thing, if you are constantly and successfully resisting temptation, you're inhuman, because no human can do it. For another thing, if you could resist all temptation, you really would fall out of grace because the only way you can fall out of grace is by not sinning. Only a manifested passion or lust can be crucified; you cannot crucify something that doesn't exist. Therefore, the passion or the lust must already have happened. Again, the question Paul is addressing here is not, "I wonder if I'll be able to keep from sinning," but, "Now that I've sinned, what am I going to do about it?" On to the next paragraph with you.

You're going to walk away from it, refuse to worry about it, then turn to Christ and contemplate Calvary. This will so severely shock the poor passion or lust that it will clamor for attention. It will say things like, *Don't you know I'm keeping you from being a good Christian? Don't you know I'm ruining God's opinion of you?* These will be lies, of course, because God's opinion of you is based upon Christ's work on the cross, not upon your behavior. But the incessant whinings of passions and lusts are irresistible bait to most Christians, and most Christians take this bait, along with the hook, the line, and that thing that makes the bait sink. This is when most Christians begin trying to kill the passion or the lust. This, of course, delights the passion or lust, because trying to kill it only gives it more power. That's why Paul did not say to kill passions and lusts, but to crucify them. I know I keep repeating myself, but I'm fighting centuries of unhappy tradition here. Remember what crucifying the passion and lust means?

Correct. Crucifying the passion or lust means that you put the tip of your thumb to the tip of your nose and then wiggle your four fingers at it, denying it what it needs to survive—your attention. (Ignoring it is better, but if you must do something, then try this nose technique.) The passion or lust, panicking now, will try everything it can think of to win your attention, including these sickening whines:

SICKENING WHINES

1) "Oh, please try to fix me!"
2) "You can't be a good Christian with *me* on board!"
3) "Become a monk, why don't you!"
4) "Get thee to a nunnery!"
5) "Go to church more—including Wednesday nights!"
6) "Come January, make thee a resolution!"
7) "Do *something*, please, before God becomes irrevocably upset."

Are you worried now about what you will do when all your sins disappear? Sheesh. How come you worry so much? Most of your sins will not disappear until God makes you sinless. This is God's wise and purposeful design. Paul wrote in another letter: "We have this treasure in earthen vessels, that the transcendence of the power may be of God and not of us" (2 Corinthians 4:7). The treasure is God's grace, and the earthen vessels you may as well call sinning vessels. If anyone on this earth could manage to stop sinning, he or she would be very proud of it. Do you see the point? To make sure that would not happen, God poured human beings into mud pots. So why are you wishing you were a Ming vase? Our beautiful vases are reserved for the future, not for now.

Now that you've stopped tending to your passions and lusts, what should you tend to instead? I've already mentioned it, but here's another dose:

"Forgetting, indeed, those things which are behind, yet stretching out to those in front—toward the goal am I pursuing for the prize of God's calling above in Christ Jesus. Whoever, then, are mature, may be disposed to this" (Philippians 3:13-15).

By minding the things that are above (Christ), rather than those which are below (flesh), our scales will tip slowly, in spite of ourselves, toward the prize of God's calling above.

GOD LOVES CALM

How to walk worthily without even trying

Reading the first three chapters of the book of Ephesians is like flying above the clouds in an airplane. Detailed in this amazing book are all the blessings I have in Christ. The Son of God is now "seated at [God's] right hand among the celestials, up over every sovereignty and authority and power and lordship, and every name that is named" (Ephesians 1:20-21), and where Christ is, there His body is also. Concerning that body, Ephesians 2:4-6 says, "He loves us, vivifies us together in Christ and rouses us together and seats us together among the celestials, in Christ Jesus."

Nowhere in scripture is there described a higher place of honor

or a greater expectation.

Still there is more. In verse nine of chapter three I read of an administration of a secret, a secret which has been concealed for eons but was revealed by the ascended Christ to the apostle Paul. The secret is that the wisdom and power of God will be made known to sovereignties and authorities among the celestials, who have yet to know it. And God's instrument for this work will be the body of Christ. The future ministry of the body of Christ, then, lies in realms now unseen—beyond Star Wars, beyond Hollywood computer animation, beyond anything that the minds of people with pocket pens and thick glasses have dared to dream.

So much for that then

Yet Ephesians 4:1-2 is, to me, the airplane hitting the side of a mountain.

I've been above the clouds, where the sun is. Below, a heavy cloudbank has carpeted my speed. Below that, the hail and the rain. The drone of the engine, in an airplane, is such a comforting sound. It's most disturbing when it stops. But it does stop—for me, anyway.

Away with the maps and instruments, there will be no need for them now. Silently now—through the cloudbank and those troubling G-forces—goes the powerless plane. In comes the rain and the frozen ice pellets.

The side of the mountain comes much too quickly, and at far too great a speed for comfort. Witnesses say that the nose hit first, followed nearly simultaneously by everything else. I tend to believe them.

I am entreating you, then, I, the prisoner in the Lord, to walk worthily of the calling with which you were called, with all humility and meekness, with patience, bearing with one another in love (Ephesians 4:1-2).

Walk worthily of the calling? Of *this* calling? You must be kidding me, Lord. God, this must be a joke. Walk worthily of what I just read? The call is so high; You wrote it that high. You wrote it higher than the rarefied peaks of heaven. You placed it among the celestials, at Your right hand. And now, among these very beings, You entreat me—with a straight face—to walk worthily of it? How? Strange that You don't say; it's a terrible lack of information, if You ask me, and right where I need it. But, really, who needs instruction in the face of so humanly impossible a task? I'll give up now, if You don't mind. Better that than trying and failing, trying and failing, trying and failing. Do You enjoy that cycle? Do You enjoy watching Your creation drowning in the vicious whirlpool of frustrated effort? Leave me out of that, please; I'm no glutton for self punishment.

It's hard to believe—truly—that You brought this exhortation to paper. You know the human frame, and You know me, specifically. You made me the way I am. You know the things I have said to You; You know the things I have done. And still, You ask this. Do You really expect it? Do You really expect me to walk worthily?

I'm telling You now: I can't deliver. I know myself. I don't mean to be disrespectful, but I do mean to be honest. At least I'm telling You this now, before the killing cycle even begins.

I will take another liberty—since I've taken so many

You made me the way I am. Do You really expect me to walk worthily?

with You—by saying that I'm tired of encounters with Your so-called people who bubble blithely and spout platitudes and clever "walk the walk" sayings with exhortations they pretend to be doing while pretending at the same time that they're anything but hypocrites, or that they have done what they say, or tried to do yesterday what they say they did, or what they've imagined they've accomplished all their lives. It's a sham, and I know that; You know it, too; the celestials know it as well. Even some of the people spouting the platitudes know it, in their darkened rooms with no one watching them while they cry out their complaint. But on they forge in the light of day, in their bright hypocrisies, unabashed. The matter with them is faith untested, I think. They glue on their smiles, Lord. As for me, I don't know the rules of that. I don't have that brand of glue, Lord. You know me better than to think I could fake self-righteousness. I won't pretend I can do anything to please You, especially after what You went through at the cross for me. You already know me, and You know Yourself. Who am I going to kid? You, Lord?

Listen, God. *Please.*

At least I can still talk to You like I did when I was a boy, like I'm doing now. Thank You, God, that I can be this honest with You. If I can't tell You my agonies, Who can I tell? You told me to enter into Your throneroom with boldness, so here I am, hear me. I'm trusting You with my trust. You withhold the lightning bolt now, as You withheld it then, because You love Me and sent Your Son to die for my sake, I know that. You've convinced me of it, which is the only reason I can speak like this. Your love is unconditional.

So help me then, please, God. *Dear Father in Heaven, please help me. I'm wretched. I can't be like You want me to; I can't be like You. Why did You even ask me? God, I'm undone.*

The allegory

I'm standing on a dock at Dover, England, looking out over the English Channel. The horizon is hazy and far away, and France lies somewhere in the distance. I am due in France, but how I'm going to get there, I haven't a clue. I have no other resource but myself.

The water of the English Channel is notoriously dangerous. It vexes channel swimmers who are already vexed simply by virtue of being channel swimmers. The weather above the channel beats and bites the water below, often sending ice pellets into the froth. There are undercurrents in here, beneath these whitecaps, that can snatch a swimmer from the surface first, then kill him or her later, beneath the waters, where the largest of fish feed.

I'm looking out at the channel, feeling weak.

Behind me are people preparing for the swim. Behind me are extraordinary athletes all slathered with grease—grease on their eyes, grease inside their noses, grease between their legs. They have performed amazing feats with barbells, these people, to which their lean and rippling muscles attest. They have vexed their taut tummies with abdominal crunches, and their hips with scissor-kicks. They are all on special diets that have included cottage cheese, broccoli and salmon patties, but never M&Ms, cheesecake and Pop Tarts. They drink twelve glasses of water a day, usually by accident. Some have done the straits at Mackinac; one man attempted Lake Erie, being rudely bumped by oil tankers that sent him weeping to his boat. One of the athletes, a woman, circumnavigated Manhattan, battling raw human sewage in the East River—and beating it.

I turn away from these aliens and their petroleum-jellied aspirations to stare again toward the distant shore; I am despondent. I despise undercurrents, have never liked them at all. I cannot find the will to even dip two toes into the channel. I cannot, in this lifetime, abandon candy-coated chocolate.

The ship

A ship approaches. Looming larger and larger, it soon docks. The swimmers behind me in their greasy sheaths fail to notice it; their goggles are fogged.

Soon, a Man emerges from the ship, grasping the railing of it and looking my way. It's the Lord, Jesus Christ! The Lord, Jesus Christ is the Captain of the ship. He has put out a plank, and now is beckoning me with a friendly pull of His hand. I happily forsake the impossible shore for the invitation of that hand. All thought of the horizon and of the invisible land beyond is gone as I board the ship at the behest of the Lord.

The spread

The big room I look into, at His invitation, is draped at all three windows, making the light in the room soft and soothing. Besides the instant relief to my soul, there is a large table to the left filled with food: bowls of fruit, some baked chicken in a pan with gravy, and many other glass bowls filled with cheese potatoes, cole slaw, and different kinds of beans.

Silverware sits to one side, in a basket. Near the silverware are cloth napkins, folded into triangles. The aroma of coffee wafts through the air; it smells especially good to me, having so recently stood on that cold, windy dock. But that scene is gone in this place of warmth, this food, this coffee, and the Captain, Who has rescued me from the horror of the channel.

"Come in and eat," He says. "Make yourself at

home." Some people say this insincerely, but this One means it, I can tell. I can tell by His tone that He desires my company. Unashamedly, then, I enter and help myself.

I don't wonder how to pick up the napkin, or how the plate should be carried, or how many forks I touch. I scoop the potatoes and the cole slaw; I try all the beans. The chicken is my favorite. There are fresh vegetables here too, for which I don't have room. But I get them on my second trip, snatching four peeled radishes, some broccoli trees, and a handful of baby carrots. I load up on onions and cucumbers, too, and a handful of olives.

The Lord watches me the whole time—He is eating, too—smiling at me. We're sitting at a table together now, looking up once in a while to see if the other is looking. He appears to enjoy my uninhibited pleasure. I notice, too, that He never asked me to remove my shoes. I think it's strange because He has such nice carpet—soft and red. And it smells so new.

The Lord is drinking coffee now because our meal

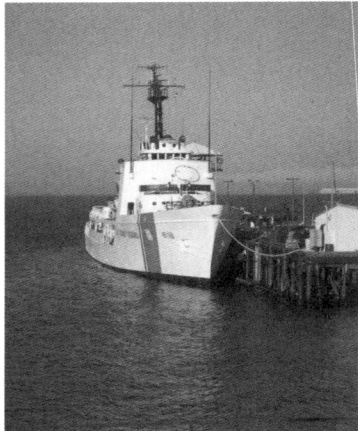

has wound down and it's time for that. The mugs are brown and very heavy, with ears perfectly accommodating the fingers; not too big, just right for the human hand. I taste in the coffee a hint of vanilla, or so it seems. I question Him about it.

"Yes," He says. "Vanilla. It's European."

"It wonderful," I say.

"So hot," says He.

"Perfect. And strong."

"I like it that way."

"Me too, Lord. I always drink it black. No spoons and things to fool with. I love this atmosphere. It's so cozy in here."

He tosses me a peanut M&M from a glass bowl at His right hand. It's not how I imagined Him to be, chucking an M&M like that, but here it comes. I catch it cleanly and pop it into my mouth. "It's always that way here," He says, and He tosses me another M&M— a red one.

The M&Ms go perfectly with the coffee. "I'm so glad You called me in," I say between crunches. "I was going crazy out there."

"I know what you mean," He says.

A minute passes. He rises, walks to a sofa and sits down. The sofa is large and soft, and He sinks deeply into it. With two taps on the cushion next to Him, He calls me beside Him.

Do you remember how it was when you were a child, and your parents—maybe your mother—called you next to her to look at a photo album? You reminisced and laughed, and maybe there was a bowl of popcorn there between you, and a bottle of Coke for a treat. And you felt cozy and warm next to your mother—next to her warm shoulder which you were touching—and your heads came together above the album to make a wonderful memory. Well, it is that way with the Lord and me, except the photo album is the Bible, and the photos from the family vacation are the book of Ephesians instead.

"Have you considered this book?" He asks. "It's a treasure."

"Oh, yes," I say. "I've done it. It's a treasure, all right. It boggles the mind."

"And takes the spirit soaring."

"Yes. Like the first three verses of chapter one."

He reads: "Blessed be the God and Father of our Lord Jesus Christ, Who blesses us with every spiritual blessing among the celestials, in Christ, according as He chooses us in Him before the disruption of the world, we to be holy and flawless in His sight, in love designating us beforehand for the place of a son."

"Incredible," I say.

"And it's only the beginning."

"I know."

He runs His finger, slowly and gracefully down the page, stopping at verse seven. "He delivers us in accord with the riches of His grace, which He lavishes on us; in all wisdom and prudence making known to us the secret of His will, in accord with His delight, which He purposed in Him, to have an administration of the complement of the eras, to head up all in the Christ, both that in the heavens and that on the earth, in Him in Whom our lot was cast also, being designated beforehand according to the purpose of the One Who is operating all in accord with the counsel of His will, that we should be for the laud of His glory, who are pre-expectant in the Christ."

I shake my head in wonder. "What a mouthful. Paul was full of what You told him there. It's like he didn't know where to stop. It's like he had to get it all out before it vanished." I pause, and my mood changes. "I know it's wonderful, but it's too big for me to completely understand. I think I understand that the body of Christ—Your body—will help to head up the universe. And that it was set apart beforehand for this purpose. It's such a burst of words; there's so much there. But I thank God that it's there, and that it's for me."

We talk more about this book of Ephesians, about the body completing Christ, Who completes God, Who completes the universe. We talk about being seated together with Christ among the celestials—the most powerful beings existent—and about how the right hand of

God is the most supreme place of power in the universe, and that that's where Christ sits and where His body sits with Him. We talk about the job of the body, to display the transcendent riches of His grace. We talk about the secret of chapter three, of the wisdom of God, of the need of distant and estranged creatures to understand and be blessed by Christ's work at Calvary.

He never takes me beyond my mind, beyond my rational thinking. When the revelations begin to stretch and trouble me, He pours more coffee, tosses me another M&M, and then sits silently. A clock ticks in the background. So sometimes there is talk, and sometimes there is silence. But all the while there is the ticking of a clock somewhere that I can't see—a clock that can be heard sometimes and sometimes not, but never seen.

The revelation

Our talk has brought us to chapter four. And when I see that chapter number, and the first verse of the chapter, it all comes back to me. It comes back to me what I had said to Him, in my agony. It comes back to me of how I'd told Him I'd given up. It comes back to me of standing on the shore fearing the cold, choppy water. It comes back to me of how distant the shore seemed. Everything comes back, of how I had failed to please Him again and again.

My face reddens, and so I turn away to stare at the table. The clock becomes audible again.

"What's wrong?" He asks. "Is something troubling you?"

I wait a few moments, wondering if I should tell Him. But He already knows. It's only because I know He knows that the boldness comes. Courage enters me as I remember that He reads hearts and that He knows mine already. It's embarrassing, this boldness, but it's liberating at the same time. The clock fades into silence again as I turn to Him.

"It's chapter four, verse one. 'Walk worthily of the calling with which you were called, with all humility and meekness, with patience, bearing with...'"

Hot tears now stream down my face. I take off my glasses and put my face in my hands. I can no longer look at Him, so I speak from inside my hands.

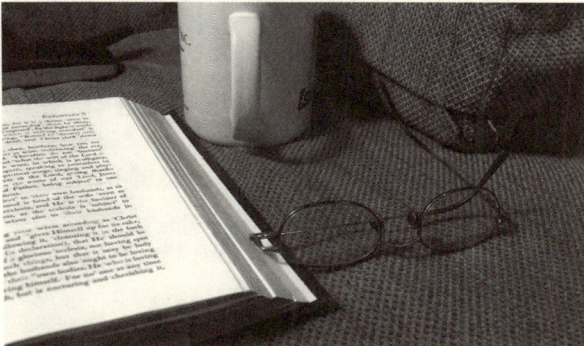

"'...bearing with one another in love...' I can't do it. I can't walk this walk, Lord. I can't walk worthily of what we've just been talking about. It's impossible for me. Maybe others can do it. Maybe Paul could do it. But I'm not Paul. He saw visions; I haven't seen anything. I'm not an apostle. I'm not a disciple. You know what I've said to You. You know the things I've done. You know what I'm like. I don't even know why I'm here."

Tick goes the clock. Twenty ticks; I count them.

He gets up from the sofa.

"I want to show you something, Martin." I look up. He stretches a little, then ascends the seven steps to the door where we first entered. "Come here, Martin," He says again. "I have something to show you."

I wipe my eyes on my sleeve, pick up my glasses and follow Him. He is walking out to the railing now, looking up and out.

I follow Him. The sun is out and I squint into it. It's much warmer now than when I first entered. A man stands on the dock, holding a rope. The Lord waves to Him.

"Bonjour!" says the man to the Lord.

WHILE SMOKING A CIGARETTE 101

"Bonjour!" says the Lord.

I stand at the railing of the boat, gripping the railing with both hands, and I feel the Lord looking at me. Things are happening to me several seconds slower than they usually happen. I do not hear the man say "bonjour" until after he has said it, maybe five seconds after. But then I do hear it. And when I hear it, I turn with the energy of a young man, of one who has new and strange vitalities surging through his body. I turn to look behind us. *Behind* us.

For what lies behind us is a channel—a cold, choppy channel of unpredictable weather and undercurrents.

What is behind us is Dover, England.

The man on the dock is a Frenchmen.

"We're there!" I shout. I am jogging along the railing now, trying to find a better place to look, to look as far as I can behind us, to make sure.

"We're in France!" I shout. I run back to the Lord. "We're across the channel! How...how did this happen? *When* did it happen?" He is still holding onto the railing with both hands, looking out over France. I see from His profile that He is smiling. Now He turns toward me and speaks.

"As soon as you stepped into the ship with Me," He says, "we set out. You didn't even notice because you were enjoying everything so much. You were eating the chicken, the potatoes, the fruits and vegetables, even

My special dessert. I loved watching you. You were drinking My coffee, enjoying My conversation. We were looking at the Word together. I enjoyed that, and so did you. And you liked the atmosphere so much. Remember? You called it 'cozy.' You reveled in the deep things we looked into."

"It was pure fellowship."

"Yes. And all that time, while we were fellowshipping, we were moving toward this shore."

I shake my head, laughing. "I can't believe this. I mean, I *can* believe this, but...I didn't even *know* it. I had no *idea* we were moving. I had no *idea* we had set out."

"Before you even sat down," He says, "we had set out."

Now He stood up straight, walked over to me, grasped both of my shoulders in His soft, firm hands, and stared into me. I could not avoid His gaze now, and neither did I want to. It was so loving. Tears formed in my eyes.

"Remember this, Martin, and do not forget it: You follow Me. You tend to Me. Eat from My table, drink from My cup, converse with Me in My Word. Enjoy yourself in My company...*and I, I will take care of the walk!*"

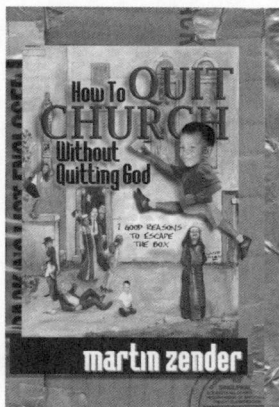

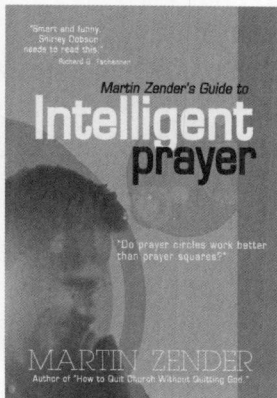